Linn Random's Guide to

Reincarnation Journey of the Soul

By

Linn Random

Copyright © Linn Random 2021

Cover Artist: DesignerHala at FiverR.com
Editor: Paige Lawson

Release date: 03/11/2021

This book is dedicated to my son Michael, my daughter-in-law, Elisabeth, my sister Sandy and my husband, Chris.

I also want to acknowledge the Archangels who work with me daily: Archangels Michael, Raphael, Metatron, Azrael, Ariel, and to all the Fairies and Guides who all have inspired me in life and along the way as I worked on this book.

This book is also dedicated to you, the reader, for whom this book was written.

Content

Preface- My Journey

"It's God's will," a church friend told me as I cried over the loss of my baby girl.

The pain was excruciating and burned through my veins like a wild fire desperate to find escape. While I hear her words, I was at a loss to grasp their meaning. Every fiber, every cell in my being was screaming, *not my God.* I was convinced that my God, this God of love and compassion would not take my child from me.

During that time in my life, I was far from perfect but I worked at it. If the church doors were open, I was there. I was there Sunday morning for Sunday School, remained for Church and returned for the Sunday service. Tuesday, I gathered with the ladies for Bible Study and Wednesday I was at the midweek service. Thursday evening, I lifted my voice in choir practice. Saturday night, I facilitated the church's youth group. In-between, I prayed and prayed and prayed. No alcohol touched my lips, I never uttered a profanity and for the most part, no impure thoughts crossed my mind.

I didn't fully buy into the hell and brimstone messages I heard at church services nor did I believe unbaptized babies went to hell. It just didn't resonate within me as truth.

And so, at that time I had lived a very dedicated life to the church, to Jesus and to God. Surely, I thought, my devotion would be moderately rewarded, instead, my baby girl was taken from me.

It didn't matter she passed in the womb; I had given her a name and, in my mind and heart she was real. I had watched her take her first steps into my arms and waved goodbye to her the first day of elementary school. Every moment had already been documented in my daydreams.

Now she was dead without ever having taken the first breath of life.

A few godly church members told me; she wasn't real. Ask any mother who has lost a child in the womb and I assure that, to each, the child is real. Erin was real to me.

I was lost after her death, unable to find my way out of the darkness of what would be life without her. There was no comfort, no solace, no peace or sleep in my world. There was no end to my suffering.

Telling me, it was God's will just didn't make sense. It didn't. There had to be another answer. There had to be!

For months, I grieved for my child. My husband and the Doctor tried to remedy my melancholy with a myriad of numbing drugs. I took them and fell into an emotional abbess where only Erin and I existed, or more accurately, did not exist. Weeks turned into months and then one day the life force within me began to awaken and slowly I fought my way back to life.

I didn't hate God for taking my child. I wanted to understand why. Why me? Why my child?

I began my quest for an answer. I was certain I would find peace at the end of my journey and a way to Erin.

It was by accident I stumbled across the book, *The Search for Bridey Murphy*, written by amateur hypnotist Morey Bernstein.

It was the story of a Colorado housewife, Virginia Tighe who in a hypnotic session spoke of her life as a 19th-century Irishwoman, Bridey Murphy. Virginia Tighe stated she was born on December 20, 1798, in Cork, Ireland. She, as Bridey Murphy, recounted her ordinary life in remarkable detail. She even spoke of being a spectator at her own funeral.

I was fascinated with her story and reread the book several times as I tried to understand her experience. I don't recall the next books I read but I continued in my pursuit for answers.

I did not leave God behind in this journey. I felt His love ever urging me onward.

My first milestone came when I could no longer argue against the theory of reincarnation. I did not need to prove it to others, I only had to prove it to myself.

For me, reincarnation explains life, relationships and the lessons we encounter and learn.

Reincarnation is about God, the Universe's unfolding plan and the journey of my soul. Erin's soul. Our Souls.

This book is an acumination of over 40 years of my study and my research. I now share this information with you.

If you are a devout reincarnationist, I will give you tools to explain it to others and strengthen your beliefs. If you do not believe in reincarnation, that's okay too; you will at least understand it.

I will be sharing my own reincarnation experiences as examples to help you understand. I invite you to explore these concepts with me.

In my world, reincarnation makes sense. We are not born to live a few decades on earth before going to a heaven or a hell. We are eternal. All part of God.

I didn't invent reincarnation. I am a believer.

Chapter 1
World View of Reincarnation

The word Reincarnation comes from the Latin word "to be made flesh again".

Reincarnation is the belief that after the body dies, we return to the spirit realm to be reunited with our loved ones before reincarnating into a new life and different body. Reincarnation is the belief in life after life after life.

There are certain religions, such as Hinduism and Buddhism, that hold this tenant as a cornerstone of their faith.

The early Christian church believed in reincarnation until the Council of Nicaea in 325 A.D. At the time, Christianity was a fledging and very fragile new religion. To stem the quarrels and in-fighting amongst the various factions, the Roman Emperor Constantine gathered the church leaders and formed an ecumenical council known as the First Council of Nicaea.

The objective of the council was to formulate a common core of beliefs. After much debate, the Holy Fathers set forth a statement of faith known as the Apostles' Creed. They chose the holy days for Christian observances and established canon law.

They also removed any reference to reincarnation which at that time was a common belief held by Christians.

The Second Council of Nicaea met in 553 A.D. This time, the Council proclaimed that the belief in reincarnation was heresy and punishable by death.

No reason was ever presented as to why the belief in reincarnation was removed. One could surmise that the church would have greater control over the people and their money. If the populace believed in reincarnation, they wouldn't feel the need to tithe the church or pay for extra services such as buying their way out of purgatory or hell. If people understood karma carried its own consequences, they would not need a confessional and would think twice before harming one another.

The Council of Nicaea also removed seven books from the Bible that conflicted with their newly pressed tenets and doctrines. The books that were eliminated contained information about Jesus' childhood, his siblings, reincarnation, and spiritual truths taught in the first few centuries of Christianity. Four scriptures on reincarnation remained in the New Testament.

The first appearance of reincarnation occurred when Jesus and his disciples came upon a blind man. They asked Jesus, "Rabbi, who sinned, this man or his parents, that he was born blind?"

His disciples were asking if the man was born blind due to his own actions in a previous life or was, he born blind because of his parent's deeds or actions. KJV, John 9:1-3.

In King James Version, Luke 9:20, Jesus asked his disciples, "Whom do the people say I am?"

Jesus asked because it was prophesized in KJV, Malachi 4:5 that God would send a messenger to prepare the way before the Messiah's return.

The disciples answered. "Some say that thou art

John the Baptist, some, Elias; and others, Jeremias, or one of the prophets.'" KJV Matthew 16:13-19.

The disciples shared that many believed Jesus to be the reincarnation of the Prophet Elijah or Jeremiah. KJV, John 1:21

Jesus answered them by saying. "But I say unto you, that Elijah is come already, and they knew him not." Matthew 17:12, KJV. Jesus was referring to John the Baptist.

I want to interject that we live in a world of invisible and universal laws. These laws, work for everyone without exception. Two examples of these universal laws are the Law of Gravity and the Law of Centrifugal Force. Both laws work equally for everyone. Therefore, one must conclude, if reincarnation works for one, it must work for all.

In another instance, Jesus and the disciples, came upon a Pharisees, named Nicodemus. The disciples asked, "How can a man be born when he is old? Can he enter the second time into his mother's womb, and be born?" John 3:3 New American Standard Bible.

Jesus replied, "Truly, truly, I tell you, no one can see the kingdom of God unless he is born again."

Lastly, I point to the statement that Jesus said, "In my Father's house are many rooms; if it were not so I would have told you. I am going to prepare a place for you." John 14:2, KJV.

Jesus was not speaking of literal mansions. He was speaking of our physical bodies which are referred to as the temples of our souls. 1st Corinthians 6:19.

Reincarnation was not a new concept during the

time of Christ, nor did it develop in India as many people believe.

`   References to reincarnation can be found in Norse legends and Germanic paganism.

Reincarnation appeared in Greek texts around 700 B.C. and plays a central role in Buddhism and Hinduism. It also surfaces in Jainism and Sikhism, two faiths that grew out of Hinduism.

The Yoruba and Edo Tribes of western Africa once believed they would be reborn into the same families as their own future descendants. The Zulu people once held the belief that a person's can be reborn as human or as different animals.

The Inuit populations that inhabit the Arctic regions of Greenland, Canada and Alaska also believe they can be reborn as humans or animals. They believed that an individual's incarnation depends on the way he or she lived and treated others.

I believe that we do not incarnate from an intellectually higher species to a one of lesser intelligence. I do believe the choice to return is ours and our decision to return is based on the lessons we choose to undertake.

In the last century, the concept of reincarnation was re-introduced to the western world by the transcendentalism movement that grew in the late 1820s and 1830s in the eastern United States.

In the 1930s the concept of reincarnation was again introduced to the world-by-world renowned psychic Edgar Cayce, known as The Sleeping Prophet.

The interest in reincarnation was jump-started in recent times through the teachings and books by Betty J. Eadie, Dr. Brian Weiss, Dick Sutphen and other New Age philosophers and religious leaders.

Today approximately 30 million Americans believe in reincarnation. More than half of the world's population shares this belief. Many people believe that number is actually higher.

I find no conflict with the teaching of Jesus or other religious leaders who advise mankind to be tolerant, kind to others with the warning that what you send out comes back multiplied.

.   To understand this philosophy is to understand how karma holds us responsible for our lives and how we teach others.

We come here, to this earth plane, to balance our karma, understand the lessons of life, love and forgiveness with the ultimate goal of unification with God.

We return to new cycles of life after life after life.

Chapter 2
The Cycle of Life after Life after Life

We came into this world by traveling through a dark passageway and we were met with earthly light. In most cases, we were welcomed by Doctors, medical professionals and by loving parents, grandparents and others who were there waiting to care for us. At the end of our journey, we once again travel through a dark tunnel to the light of the spirit realm where souls are also waiting to welcome us and help us transition to the spiritual world.

This is our circle of life. We do not die. We leave our heavy human bodies behind and like all organic matter, they turn to dust. When we make our transition, we once again become our celestial selves, for this is who we really are.

The Law of Thermodynamics states energy can neither be created nor destroyed. Using water as an example of this law, when water is frozen, it is ice. Heat the ice and it changes form to become liquid. Boil the water and it vaporizes into steam. If you capture the steam and allow it to cool, it will reform into liquid once again. In a matter of speaking, we do the same for we are energy and spirit.

On this planet, we are at our heaviest. As we transition, we become lighter as we return to our true form which is the spirit. Throughout the process of change, our energy changes form, but it never ceases to exist. Our souls are eternal.

Thanks to the dedication of author and researcher,

Dr. Raymond A. Moody, we know more of what this transition looks like through his acclaimed work on NDE, Near Death Experiences.

From Dr. Moody NDEs studies, with very slight variations, when we leave our worldly bodies, most NDE's first describe a sensation of momentarily floating above our bodies. In these first few seconds, NDEs can view their bodies from a location in the room.

Some NDEs observe lifesaving procedures performed by medical professionals. Others say they leave the room and wander about hospital corridors eavesdropping on conversations. When they return from their NDE experiences, they accurately recount conversations they heard or life-sustaining measures they observed.

During these first few moments of our transition from this world to the spirit realm, a dark tunnel appears and opens to us. At the end of this tunnel is an exquisite light that beacons to us. We travel quickly into the light to find loved ones and friends who have passed over are waiting for us.

They are also greeted by a compassionate being who some identify as Jesus, Buddha, an Angel or Deity of their faith. The experience is the same for all; no matter the beliefs, religion or creed of the individual. Atheists who have gone through a NDE experience return as believers and describe their NDE experience the same way.

NDEs describe being engulfed in an encompassing consciousness of love and compassion that surrounds them completely.

At this point, some are simply told, it is not their

time or their mission is not complete. Mothers of small children express a desire to return. What follows is an immediate and sometimes abrupt return to their bodies.

Some have shared they experienced a life review. I did.

From my earthly perspective, I dreaded the thought of a life review. Even though I do my best to live a kind, compassionate life, I knew I fell short. I could only assume my review be harsh and conclude in judgement and condemnation. That is not what happened.

In my life review, I stood in the center of a group of judges perhaps counselors would be a better designation. Together, we watched my life in review.

My attention was drawn to a 3D holographic movie of my life. The imagery had far more depth than any manmade hologram as it was rich in depth, infused with energy and emotion. As my story unfolded, I watch my life with a what I can only describe as a detached curiosity.

My life unfolded before me, but I viewed it through the prism of my emotions as well as experiencing the thoughts and feelings of others who shared my life journey. Instead of the judgement or severe condemnation I had expected, I watched without guilt and joined in on soft critiques on circumstances in my life where I could have done better.

As I watched three emotional Tsunamis washed over me. The first tidal surge of sensations was my own emotions as I interacted with others. The second emotional flood weighted me with the hurts and pain I had caused others as well as the intensity of my own anger, resentment, envy and the judgments I had held not only of myself but of others. This flash of emotional memory was crushing. Not only did I bear witness to my own negative reactions but I could see how I had affected others. I could only marvel at the precious moments of wasted time I spent in negative thoughts or actions, whether they were accident or intentional.

The last and final cascade of emotional deluge that flowed over me and through me was the overwhelming experience of gratitude and love I had received from others. It was this last experience that stayed with me and lingered after the life review. My review concluded with immense feelings of gratitude for the life I had lived and the lessons I had learned.

Throughout my life's story, not once was I shown my alcaides, awards or achievements. They didn't even receive an honorable mention. Instead, I viewed a forgotten kindness of a small moment when I had helped a disabled woman mail a letter or of the times, I offered help to strangers. Our goodness, the kindness and love we show others are the important acts of our life story.

There was no mention of hell, or damnation, no whisper of condemnation and no judgment. I received offerings and suggestions on how I could have improved in my interactions with others. I was left with an overwhelming sense of love and gratitude for my life and those who had shared it with me.

Betty J. Eadie best describes this same type of experience in her book, *Embraced by the Light*.

I urge you to read Betty J. Eadie's book, *Embraced by the Light*, and any book authored by the fabulous Dr. Raymond Moody, especially his book, *Life After Life*. Both authors changed my life and my perception on how to live it.

Moving forward from the life review, we have an opportunity to rest, watch and visit our loved ones on earth. If we choose, we can attend what I can only describe as a university-style educational system or explore other worlds of extraordinary beauty and life.

There is no time in this world, this afterlife. Time is a finite thing that we use here in the physical world and on this our planet is the only place we experience time.

After a period of growth or exploration, we can choose to remain in the spirit realm, volunteer to serve as guides and assist earthbound people or we can choose to reincarnate.

If we choose to reincarnate, we often incarnate with our soul group.

What we learn is that life is eternal. There is no death. While our physical bodies return to dust, our souls live on to learn new lessons, repeating cycles of birth and rebirth as we move in an upward spiral ever closer to God.

In the following chapter, we will explore, evaluate and discover, the lessons we chose to experience and understand in Earth School.

Chapter 3
Earth School- Choosing to Reincarnate

Earth School. As hard as it is to understand, you made the choice to return to this planet, and you came with a plan. You came to resolve karmic debts and to learn an array of lessons born out of living, loving and forgiving.

You were not born to be the victim of circumstances but to rise above them. The lesson is complete when you forgive all involved which includes yourself and then release the experience.

That which you do not forgive and release in peace, you are destined to repeat. Welcome to Earth! This whole planet is our university, our Earth School, which was created for our highest good.

Before you incarnated to this planet, you met with a group of highly skilled Karmic counselors or masters. Together, you planned a life with three to five major lessons as well as a host of minor challenges. You also tied your life and lesson plan with other members of your soul group as you linked your life and lessons with theirs.

You fashioned a magnificent tapestry that interlocked your past lives with the karmic lessons you chose to undertake in your new life.

We often choose to incarnate with the same group over many lifetimes. Sometimes a new soul will arrive and be with us for just one lifetime. They do so as their life choices align with ours.

We were not born into this life to accomplished a grand tasks such as to write the great American novel but to experience love, endure pain and heartache so we can rise above our life lessons by release them, thus balancing our karma.

Karma is not always about punishment; it can also be about reward. I sometimes wonder if my simple acts of kindness return to me as a parking space closer to the mall entrance. Being kind to others is more than its own reward, your kindness will return multiplied.

You are not the victim of life but the victor as you outgrow your experiences in love.

If you are unhappy with this concept, think about it, understanding will come.

Not all karma originated in a past life, some you caused in this life.

The good news is when you forgive each person including yourself and release the experience, the lesson does not repeat, in this life or a future experience.

I believe it is the highest form of love and sacrifice is to have a companion soul step up and volunteer to be our teacher in a hard lesson. I resisted this concept for years until I saw the wisdom of it.

I encourage you to look back across your life to uncover any unhappy patterns, romantic entanglements to find the lessons and forgive and release all involved in such experiences.

Lessons are not confined to personal relationships

as some of our lessons appear with unpleasant bosses or coworkers. There is a lesson for you if you encounter the same type of difficult relationship with a supervisor or problematic coworker; same unpleasant personality types but at different companies. These challenges give you opportunities to grow so you never have to deal with their types again.

It is my wish that you experience only happy personal lives in which you are always financially successful.

If you have a loving and supportive relationship, I am thrilled for you. A healthy relationship tells me that you and your partner have risen above many relationship issues and are now together to experience new challenges and adventures.

As we review our lives, we realize that certain experiences were part of our life's plan. Be aware, not every circumstance was prearranged. Some you created in this lifetime.

When you make the choice to return to Earth School, you can choose your family. You can select a physicality that makes you a super-star athletic. You decide your body type as well as bring with you any of your likes, dislikes, or fears you had in a previous life. You choose what innate talents or gifts needed to help you achieve your goals. Many hobbies and pleasurable pastimes are born from previous lives and you can choose to enjoy them again.

You choose your gender, race or perhaps to experience life in a different social or economic class. You can choose where to live. All decisions are made to best serve your spirit's evolution, compliment the life you want to live and the lessons you want to learn.

You can choose your parents and make your life choices based on your parents' career. For example, if you want to be an actor, you can choose parents who are in the film industry. If you plan to become a doctor, lawyer, educator or singer you can chose parents who are already well-established in those fields.

Not all children born into such families follow their parents' path but it increases the odds of professional success when choosing one's parents.

You are by no means limited to experience your life with the same family group. You can choose to experience life with a new group. It is always your choice.

Edgar Cayce shared that millions of souls who have chosen to reincarnate at this time have had previous lifetimes in Atlantis. Some of those with Atlantean ties have a fascination with all things Atlantis and with crystals.

Your soul yearns to experience a variety of different scenarios, economic conditions, social status as well as religious and spiritual beliefs.

You chose Earth School to learn.

Many have shared with me; they do not remember past lives. I assure the memories are there, hiding in plain sight. You left breadcrumbs to find and discover.

In the next chapter, I'll show you where to find the breadcrumbs you left behind.

Chapter 4
The Bread Crumbs You Left Behind

Many people have shared with me that they have no recollection of past lives. This is not true for throughout your life; you have stumbled across the breadcrumbs you left behind.

You may recall when you had a flash memory over a place or event but you simply dismissed the moment as an odd happenstance or curious phenomena. You never took the time to examine those tiny fragments, those memories, you stumbled upon.

I urge you to look back in to those moments and remember them now.

As you reflect on those memories or déjà vu experiences, you will wonder why you were so quick to initially dismiss them.

A client of mine is forever posting pictures of female warriors on horseback. Over and over, she is drawn to these images like a relentless moth to an irresistible flame. She never posts horses grazing in a pasture or woodland trails; she's consistently drawn to women mounted on horseback or holding a lance while being driven in a chariot. Without realizing her obsession with these images, she is staring at forgotten memories of a former life.

Accessing her Akashic Records, it came as no surprise to discover she had lived a past life as Boudica, Queen of the Iceni. This legendary warrior Queen mobilized a massive army to fight the Romans in 60 A.D.

Recently a male client swore to me that he had no recollection of a past life. As we began to talk, this city boy, told me of his lifelong fascination with the night sky and his love of open water. An avid hunter and outdoorsman, he shared he felt most at home when he sits before an open campfire. In a past life regression, he discovered he was once a Viking who navigated by the stars. In another life, he lived as a mountain man in 1830s and 1840s in the American Rockies. In that life, he was married to a beautiful native American, who is his companion in this lifetime.

Many children and adults with no reason or cause, at least in this lifetime, have unreasonable fears of fire, heights, water or thunder. They express extreme anxiety at the sight of a flickering flame, the distant sound of thunder or tight spaces.

One night, I was passively watching a television documentary when a Viking longboat was appeared on the screen. The sight of this impressive vessel sent shock waves through me. My body shook. My throat went dry. And, I was visibly shaken for hours.

After three days of being unable to shake the image, I did a past-life regression in the hopes of releasing this startling and terrifying image. In my regression, I was transported to Lindisfarne Abbey in 793, where I served as a monk. I died at the hands of a Viking berserker. My death was grotesque, brutal and savage. The memory of a Viking longboat triggered a long ago and until that moment forgotten memory.

Once I visited a friend whose home was filled with

Titanic memorabilia. This was about 15 years before the Titanic movie was released so finding so many Titanic collectibles was quite remarkable. One of the most significant finds was a newspaper account of the tragedy with the glaring headline, *"Titanic Sinks, 1500 Passengers Die."* She had preserved the newspaper and it was the first thing she saw when she entered her home. She had a replicator of a Titanic life preserver by her pool and several models of the luxury liner were scattered about her house. She was obsessed with all things Titanic. Even a nonbeliever could make the connection between her fascination with the Titanic born from her own memories of her past life as one of its passengers on that ill-fated voyage.

The French term déjà vu means "already seen." It's the uncanny feeling that even though you have never been to a location or place before, it feels familiar.

Déjà vu experiences occur when you find yourself on a European street or step onto a battlefield you have never visited before. A sensation washes over you and you may have even remarked to a companion at the time that you felt you had been at this place before.

Instead of exploring the feeling, you dismissed it, owning the sense of familiarity to dream or a movie you saw. You never took the time to recognize this as a memory of a past life experience.

People are sometimes drawn to cast-iron toys at yard sales or you may linger over a Victorian desk discovered at an antique shop. These items are strangely memorable but you don't recall seeing this furniture style in your present experience.

You may have found yourself unable to take your

eyes away from an artifact in a museum, or you stare a bit too long at a chipped piece of pottery bowl unearthed near an ancient burial site. You are drawn to these items as you may have touched them or used them many years ago in another place or another life.

We have all met new friends or lovers with whom we have an instant connection. Our initial meetings are so familiar and so comfortable; it seems like we have known them all our lives.

Talents and skills can also be clues from a previous lifetime.

As a teen, I picked up a bow and arrow left from my Uncle's Boy Scout meeting. The bow felt natural in my hands and without ever having touched a bow before, I perfectly framed an arrow and released it with surprising accuracy. My Uncle marveled at my skill. Either he nor I realized at the time, I had lived a life as a master of the English longbow in service to the King.

As a child, I naturally took to the back of a horse. I possessed an agility and balance that far surpassed riders twice my age. This talent, this skill was but yet another breadcrumb left by my lifetimes when I had ridden in mounted warfare.

I share my personal stories with you to help you awaken to your own past.

Look back on your life to skills and memories you once dismissed as coincidence or innate talent, to friends and lovers who were oh so familiar at first meetings and to places you felt you had once walked before.

Write down these déjà vu experiences.

Your talents, your interests and perhaps even your career choices are telltale signs of your past lives.

They are but memories, the bread crumbs you left behind.

Chapter 5
Children & Past Lives

We were having coffee with a friend, when he said with a grin, "I don't know what to do with that kid of mine."

With a shake of his head and explained, "Yesterday, Andy asked me, how come you are so big when before, I was big and you were little?"

A knowing look passed between my husband and I. We knew 4-year-old Andy was remembering a past life.

It is not uncommon for children between the ages of 2 to 6 years old to innocently share memories of previous lives. Sometimes, their parents find their words alarming while the majority simply dismiss their remarks. Past life memories children share will generally fade as the child embraces his or her current life.

Between ages 2 to 6, children may ask odd questions or make extraordinary statements such as "Where's my other Mommy?" or "Look Daddy, that's where I lived before." Children will also openly share comments like, "Mommy, it's okay if I paint? I was a painter before."

I have heard many stories of children reacting to thunder as a soldier would respond to a mortar attack.

If your child makes such an assertion, offer a soft reply. If you want to explore their comments, do so very gently by asking open-ended questions such as "Do you remember anything else?" or "That must have been scary".

A child may express a fear of losing a parent or a memory of a time when they were left alone. If that is the case, assure the little one by saying, "That was a long time ago; I promise to never leave you now." Children want to feel loved and safe.

Not all past lives bubble to the surface as pleasant memories. Children wake up in the middle of the night from scary dreams. Their childhood nightmares can be centered around bad guys chasing them. Children may exhibit eccentric phobias. As a child, my sister refused to eat coconut, we still do not know why, but she insisted it wiggled. Perhaps her assertion came from a time when she was forced to eat contaminated food to survive.

If your child makes such a comment, acknowledge it and offer a brief explanation. Write down their statement so you can share them when the child is old enough to understand.

Do not push them into remembering facets of a previous life or attempt to hypnotize them. Reincarnation is complicated for adults. Children should never be encouraged or hypnotized into remembering past life. These memories will eventually take them to sufferings and deaths in previous lives. Instead, encourage children to focus on their current life.

Children often act out past lives through play and may gravitate toward certain toys. Many times, these interests offer clues of past life experiences.

Looking back at my childhood, I recall the neighborhood boys playing soldier. Dressed in WWII battle gear and clutching toy guns to their sides, they feverishly weaved in and around trees, cars and trash bins. I see now they were reenacting a past lives of World War II combat.

As a toddler, I was overly obsessed with books. Between 5 and 6-years-old, I wrote a series of books that my mother dutifully bound in brown paper bags. They are quite amusing now but I can see my interest was born from past vocations as an author, scribe or writer.

My son from an early age was overly fascinated with all things Japanese. His interest went far beyond the Power Rangers and Pokémon to a near obsession with Japanese culture. He went through a phase when he insisted on using chopsticks at every meal. His favorite place at Disney's Worlds Showcase was the Japanese Pavilion. His interest in Japan continued through his teen years and as a newlywed, he and his bride traveled to Tokyo.

What were your interests as a child? What are your children drawn to? Perhaps some of your or your children's pursuits were from a past life occupations.

Some children will express an interest in a particular profession. My sister's favorite pastime was extending medical care to her dolls. Eventually, she pursued a career as a nurse.

Some children enter this world with a birthmark. In a past life regressions, they sometimes discover that their birthmark is linked to an injury from a previous life.

One of the biggest indicators of past life abilities comes to us through child prodigies. History is alive with children who possess a natural talent or proclivity to extraordinary gifts. These child prodigies bring with them a highly demonstrative talent and skill.

Today you can find stories and books about children who claim to be a reincarnation of actors, sports figures, or notable personages such as the Dali Lama.

These children are able to identify pictures of their former adult selves and also are able to name aunts, uncles, parents, grandparents and friends.

One child claimed to be the reincarnation of a legendary 1920s professional golfer. It's interesting to note when compared to this golfer, the young prodigy precisely mimics the golfer's swing and follow-through.

Mozart was such a prodigy who played the harpsichord at 4, was composing music at 5 years old and was performing on the stage by 6 years of age. There are music teachers who try as they will to groom their children to mimic Mozart's skills and abilities. They give their children every advantage but through no fault of the child, they fail.

Where did Mozart and other child prodigies gain their talent? Nature, nurture or did they bring their amazing talent from a past life when they performed as skilled pianists, world class golfers or actors with a nose for business.

Blaise Pascal, a 17-century French mathematician, physicist, and philosopher was not taught math as a child, yet he excelled at mathematics at a very young age. As an adult, he established himself as one of Europe's greatest mathemations and scientific minds.

By age 6 Hungarian-American mathematician, John von Neumann was able to joke with his father in classic Greek and demonstrated an uncanny ability as a mathematician. As an adult, Von Neumann came to be regarded as the preeminent mathematician of his time who made major contributions in mathematics, physics, economics, and science.

American industrialist Henry Ford believed in his previous life he was a soldier who died at the Battle of Gettysburg.

As a child, General George S. Patton, Jr. vividly recalled memories of fighting Turkish armies in historic battles. Throughout his life, Patton remembered his past lifetimes as a warrior and military combatant.

I want to close with the reminder that children should not be encouraged to remember past lives or regressed into recall. Record your child's comments for a time when they are old enough to understand them.

As you look at your own families, many of you will agree, there is a divine symmetry in our own relationships. In other lives, we exchanged roles with our mothers, fathers, siblings and our own children, as I shared at the beginning of this chapter. Andy was once the father of our friend and in this life, he is the son. So, it is when we incarnate within our groups. We incarnate to learn, explore and love those who love us, again.

I will share more about soul groups in a later chapter, but first, I'd like to explore with you those we call our soulmates.

Chapter 6
Soulmates

The term soulmate generally refers to a distinctive romantic partner with whom we have shared countless lifetimes.

In the New Age culture, the term soulmate is referred to as a twin flame, the mirrored image of our soul. They are yen to our yang. They make us complete.

Traditionally, one of the most popular reasons a person seeks out a psychic is because they want to know if the person, they met two minutes ago is their soulmate.

Modern-day psychologists believe one soulmate is unrealistic.

When I was younger, I bought into the romantic ideal of a single soulmate. I was sure that Tom, then Dorian and especially Marc were my soulmates, the twin to my flame. I was convinced that each one respectively was the one soul who would make me complete.

I was romantically swept away by each until, the abuse started. Like a practiced waltz, the steps of this macabre dance were so familiar to me. I easily fell into their arms and danced to their music.

Each abuser played a part in my life story. Each was a teacher with whom I had signed a soul contract before entering this world. My relationships were part of a greater lesson plan. As I failed to learn from my first opportunity, the subsequent relationships became progressively worse until I realized that the person I needed to love and honor, was me.

In time, I fought my way out of these relationships, I learned to set boundaries, created a foundation of self-esteem and worthiness. I released the energies that attracted this type of man to me.

It's very clear as I write this now but at the time, I wondered why I kept attracting this type of man into my life.

Is there a pattern in your life that seems to repeat itself? You see until the lesson is learned; these patterns and behaviors will repeat as part of your curriculum.

We balance karma through relationships. For instance, if you cheated on your partner in a past life, the two of you may reincarnate into a life where roles are reversed. By switching roles from one life to the next, we have the opportunity to understand how our actions affect others.

Soulmates are not only our life partners but also are our brothers, sisters, parents, relatives, friends or co-workers. These people know us at a deep cellular level.

I believe each of us should experience life with a loving partner who treats us with dignity, love and respect. When you enjoy such a relationship, its likely you and your partner have experienced the complications of relationships and are now ready to move onto new adventures and challenged as a couple together.

Dick Stephun has written some beautiful books on reuniting with soulmates and the reasons why we do.

In his bestseller, *You Were Born Again to Be Together*, Dick Sutphen explores soulmates and further expands on this topic in his book, *Soul Agreements*.

Edgar Cayce, The Sleeping Prophet, believed that God created our souls to be androgynous. Cayce shared we are our own soulmates with equal parts both male and female. He believed we are each our own soulmate and we reunite with our other half in the spirit realm. This resonates with me.

We choose soulmates. If you are curious about a present or past life relationship, consider doing a past life regression to uncover the reasons you are attracted to or aligned to partner.

I didn't do past life regressions with my first two relationships but I did with the third. After the third relationship, I wanted to uncover my part in the in the relationship and understand the root cause behind them. I wanted to uncover my obsession with Marc. My feelings were so much more than romantic love. He was my drug of choice. I had to know if there was something more to him and our relationship. I had to know if we had lived and loved before. We had.

In the past life regression, I was taken back to a past life in Egypt.

In our Egyptian lifetime, I was a daughter in what must have been an affluent family as we lived in a beautiful home and had servants to fulfill our every need. Marc, as I know him in this lifetime was a guard in my family's household. During that time, I stole Marc away from my sister, and we continued this back and forth with him for centuries. Ugh, what was I thinking!

Though he was no longer married when we began our relationship, at least that's what he told me, which was a lie; his current wife and then ex-wife was my Egyptian sister. I had won him again. Yeah. At the end of our relationship, he went back to her and they remarried. I was broken and left in pieces.

I was desperate to end this destructive pattern and through a life regression, I was able to forgive him, to forgive myself, find absolution and peace.

Doing a past life regression may heal a relationship as well as resolve past life relationships that carry over into this your current life.

I want to be clear, if you are in an abusive or unpleasant relationship you don't have to remain bound in one. Once you understand and see the relationship for what it is, forgive all involved and release the experience, you are freed and absolved from any Karmic debt through the Law of Grace.

The Law of Grace forgives karmic debt. You do not have to keep banging your head on the wall for the moment you recognize it hurts, and you no longer want to experience the pain, the lesson is learned. Your debt is resolved. You are free to live a beautiful life that serves your best and highest good.

When you are ready to release a relationship pattern, you heal it by forgiving all involved and rising above it through love. You will know you are "healed" when you can look on the relationship without any emotional attachment. When an issue is resolved, you will find peace and let go of all resentment, anger and blame. Left in its place you find compassion, serenity and wish this person good in their upward journey.

If you do not fully release a relationship or an experience, you are tightening your etherical cord to it. By not letting go, you are bound to repeat the situation with a new partner. Let go, release, forgive all and only then, will you will experience new different outcomes and healthy relationships.

If your soulmate or life partner makes his or her transition before you, know that it's okay to find love again. Understand, one day you will be reunited with your loved on Whether you remain a widow or widower, it's up to you. Your choice.

I want to assure you all that heaven will sing if you choose to find a new loving relationship and your beloved spouse will be leading the choir, for such is the nature of our souls.

Soulmates are truly magical part of our lives. There is a learning experience in each and every one of them.

We will continue studying soulmates and how they are intermingled with our soul group in the next chapter.

Chapter 7
Group Reincarnation

A soul group is a group of individual souls who come together life after life and agree to incarnate at the same time. The purpose of a soul group is to learn life lessons with souls who are attuned with us. Our soul groups allow us to clear karmic debts and rise above the lessons we choose to learn.

What! Are you kidding me? These people again! No way!

Before you simply reject this premise, a gentle reminder that on the other side, our sisters are not the bratty siblings that destroyed our high school yearbook or the stern father who delivered punishment. On the other side, they are beautiful, kind, loving souls who came into this life with us and with their own agenda. They came into our lives to help us in our soul's journey. They offer us the most wonderful opportunities to assist us as we balance karma from our previous lives.

We choose to incarnate together with the unified mission to help members of our soul group and fulfill our life's mission.

The roles in soul groups may change, but the game remains the same. As an example, I am the daughter of my Mother in this life as she was my daughter in a former life.

A soul group can be the family you are born into or a group of friends who gather around you and support you.

I often look about my psychic friends and know; this isn't the first time we have shared lives together.

A soul group may be made up of coworkers or cohesive teams who were reborn for a specific mission like space engineers who come together for a NASA project or an elite military unit or command.

Not all of our group members are part of the same soul group. Some join with us as they are traveling the same path with similar agendas.

Those who present our greatest life challenges are our greatest teaches. Dysfunctional families, therefore, provide us a trifecta of chaos and growth.

Through soul groups, we experience health, wealth, poverty, specific traits, habits, interests and enjoyable pastimes with members of our group.

Some who believe that we will choose to wait until everyone in our soul group has journeyed to the other side before we reincarnate. While I see the merit in this, I don't know that I totally agree as we always have free choice as to when we incarnate to this planet. I believe while it's nice when this happens, it's certainly not necessary to incarnate into the same group.

Throughout history there have been soul groups that reincarnated for great change. America was the beneficiary of one such soul group. How else can you explain Adams, Jefferson, Franklin, Washington and the signers of the American constitution, all choosing to be reborn at the time period, to fulfill America's manifest destiny? I suspect this group once discussed democracy in ancient Greece and then gathered again to sign the Magna Carta.

Not all groups were incarnated for good, some groups formed for evil. No one need look no further than the collective of men who assemble around Hitler in World War II.

Between lifetimes on earth and if we choose to re-incarnate, we begin by planning our itineraries with other members of our soul group. This amazing tapestry is highly complicated, extremely detailed and wonderous in its design.

Our unique journey is built on an advantageous platform that allows us to experience our soul's highest growth.

I believe our soul group's journey aligns in a beautiful and amazing adventure that connects us all in an ever-expanding Universe in which all members play an essential part of our story.

Group incarnations are sometimes in a state of flux as our group will expand in one lifetime and decrease in the next. This occurs as the needs of the many shift and blend into the needs of a few.

I believe we continuously change partners and roles within our soul group. The members of our soul group help us balance our karma.

We have gone through numerous lifetimes together with members of our group and they know us on a deeply cellular level. This creates a dazzling connectivity.

I believe the size of the group does not matter but the experience we bring to each other does. We are connected. All of us.

Each of us is fulfilling our role as co-creators with the Universe.

We are not alone in our journey for we bring into our lives furry and feathery friends. In the next chapter, we will look at our animal companions and the lessons they share with us.

Chapter 8
Pets & the After Life

Losing a pet can be one of the hardest and most painful experiences in our lives. I marvel at how such little things can take so much space in our hearts. The loss of a beloved pet can be as devastating as the loss of a human companion.

I am often asked if our pets reincarnate? Yes, yes and yes.

It gives us immense comfort to know and understand our pets reincarnate and sometimes return to us in the same lifetime.

Animals have shorter life spans than humans. They are our teachers and teach us lessons in unconditional love, compassion and provide us with the perfect companionship. They are here to play a significant part in the human experience.

Hollywood has picked up on this popular subject and created several beautiful movies about animal reincarnation. Recent films on this topic include A *Dog's Purpose* and A *Dog's Journey.* Both have opened many who viewed them to the theory of reincarnation. These films are faithful to a dog's love and devotion to their owners. Both movies are worth watching!

When pets make their transition, I believe they cross over the Rainbow Bridge to a heavenly domain where they chase butterflies, play with animal friends and roll about on feathery green grass and bask in divine sunlight.

Like their human counterparts, our pets watch over their owners and sometimes return home to lay on their masters' bed at night.

Horses roam with great grassy plains with herds of buffalo and elephants.

When we cross over, I believe our beloved pets are waiting by the gate to greet us. I have said often and I know many of you will agree with me, you can keep your streets of gold and mansions on the hill, I will be happy to spend my eternity across the Rainbow Bridge.

Our belief in animal reincarnation dates back in history to many ancient religions and mythology. Egyptian Pharaohs and Queens mummified their pets so they could bring them into their afterlives.

Native Americans, many African and eastern religions believe that humans can reincarnate as animals.

As stated previously, I personally do not believe we return as animals. I have no recall of any past life experiences as a dog or cat nor am I aware of anyone who has had such experiences. However, as I was writing this book, I came across several women who believed they spent their former lives as cats.

I am open to animals reincarnating into other animals but I am not sure I buy into human to animal reincarnation. This is one of those questions, I am simply going to table until I reach the other side of life.

American mystic Edgar Cayce believed the soul evolves through a succession of animal incarnations to achieve human status. I agree with this premise.

International renowned psychiatrist, Dr. Brian Weiss, the author of *Many Lives, Many Mansions*, shared his belief that pets have souls and reincarnate.

Mediumship is the practice of communication between those on this planet and loved ones who made their transition to the spirit realm. I am accustomed to hearing Mediums say, during a reading, "I see a cocker spaniel next to your loved one."

To which a relative will reply, "Oh, that's Buttons. My Grandfather never went anywhere without Buttons." It's a comfort to know our animal companions share eternity with us.

I believe dogs, as a species, have past life recall. How else can you a explain a poodle who barely leaves the house experiences fear at the sound of thunder or fireworks? I believe the fear of gunfire dates back to a time when they were either hunted or used in warfare.

There are countless books on pet reincarnation. They are all beautiful, loving stories of our pet's life after life.

It's a joy to know, that one day, we will be reunited with our fur or feathery friends.

I say again, my idea of heaven is to spend every moment of mine playing with my beloved furry companions across the Rainbow Bridge.

Chapter 9
Exploring Past Lives through Hypnotherapy

Many people undertake a past life regression to discover who they were in a previous life, understand a past life connection with their current partner or perhaps to find out if they were once a famous or infamous historical luminary.

Past life regression is a technique that uses hypnosis or a deep meditative state to access past lives. You can also learn about your past lives through your dreams, or by a flash of recollection by simply viewing a television show.

Hypnotherapy dates back to ancient Egypt. Today, hypnotherapy has been and is used in weight loss, smoking cessations, overcoming addictions, depression, phobias and even PTSD. Hypnosis can help us overcome obstacles and make changes in our behavior. We also access past lives through hypnosis.

Before you argue with me, that you can't be hypnotized, I want to share, I was that girl. My first hypnotherapist was a medical doctor who only smiled when I told him I could not be hypnotized. It took him a matter of seconds to put me into a deep hypnotic trance.

If you decide to pursue a past life regression, I'd like to suggest you first be open to the experience. Schedule an appointment with a medical professional or a licensed hypnotherapist. I'll share more of my own experiences in hypnosis and what you can expect in the next few pages.

Some people who by understanding the source cause of a pattern, fear or behavior is all that is necessary to achieve full recovery.

One of today's most prominent leaders in past life hypno-therapy is psychiatrist Dr. Brian Weiss. In his books, Dr. Weiss is able to help his patients access previous lives through a past life regression.

Medical associations as a whole, do not recommend hypnotherapy. However, hypnotherapy is not only very popular for past life regressions but demand is high.

In a past life regression, you may uncover the origin of a fear such as a fear of snakes or heights. This type of phobia could be traced back to a deadly snake encounter a century ago or it may be locked in our DNA from a time when we lived in caves.

Past life regressions answer déjà vu moments and give us a certain amount of relief as we identify and clarify those feelings.

Past life regressions won't keep you from experien-cing future heartache. They may give you the insight and patience in dealing with those you love and who love you.

A past life regression may help increase feelings of self-worth or prevent duplicating past mistakes.

Many people have shared after a past life regression, they will lose their fear of death or are able to transform grief into a confidence that one day they will be reunited with their loved ones.

Some people who have gone through a past life re-gression find talents, become motivated to change careers or are energized into trying former hobbies or interests.

One client told me; he had a calling to be a teacher. A past life regression gave him the insight and courage to pursue his dream.

If you seriously want to pursue past life regression, I recommend visiting a medical professional or licensed hypnotherapist in person. Working with someone over the phone makes me extremely nervous. I personally won't hypnotist anyone over the phone even if someone else is present in the room. I am going to explain why and issue a warning. The following may be frightening to read but I want you to understand the seriousness of undertaking a past life regression with a nonprofessional. The following is a true event.

Many years ago, a hypnotherapist was doing a past life regression with a college student in a large auditorium. When the young man slipped into a heavy Texas accent, the audience quietly chuckled. The student described his life as a cattle rustler in the old west.

Eventually, his crimes caught up with him and he was lifted onto his horse by some ranchers who put a rope around his neck. When the horse was pulled from him, he began to experience being hanged, not just in his past life, but also in his current life and before the student body. For several frantic minutes the hypnotherapist worked unsuccessfully to bring him back to the present. We all watched in horror as the student clawed at the phantom noose around his neck. Panic spread through the room. After several frantic minutes, the young man was brought back to the present and taken to the hospital where he made a full recovery.

If I have frightened you from experimenting with a hypnotic session with anyone over the phone or at a cocktail party, good. I am not going to apologize because I care about you and your safety. I want to issue you a strong warning, hypnosis is not a parlor game. Hypnosis can have very real and serious consequences.

Unless otherwise instructed, when we visit the past, we generally will travel back to the most dramatic moment of that life. For most of us, it's the moment of our death. That's why people remember their deaths, not the first time they saw the King.

If you are interested in having a hypnotherapy session, I am pleased to share my experiences. I have been hypnotized by different Doctors or licensed hypnotherapists in different areas of the country. The following is an example of what you might expect. There may be slight variations but the professionals who worked with me, followed the same basic techniques.

Before you schedule an appointment, read the reviews. If you can get a personal referral, do so.

You will meet the doctor or medical professional at their office, preferably during daytime hours. After a few minutes of chat, they will dim the lights and ask you to concentrate on an object in the room. Their practiced voice will be soothing

The hypnotherapist will give you instructions designed to get you into a meditative state. They may ask you to raise your arm, you are giggling at this point as you feel your arm raise on its own accord. Though you will be in a deep state of relaxation, you are conscious and in control of your body and the experience.

The hypnotherapist will progressively take you into a deeper hypnotic or meditative state and direct you to go to a time when you were happy and content in your past life.

The hypnotherapist will ask general questions such as what are you wearing or what activities people do you see. You will see these images in your mind's eye and respond accordingly. The images you see will help you identify where and when you lived in the past.

If your session is about the time and place where you first met your current life partner, they will direct you to that meeting. If your question is regarding an issue with money, the hypnotherapist work with you to reveal when that financial issue began.

Once you get to the wellpoint of when your issue with money or perhaps a first meeting with your partner occurred, the hypnotherapist will ask you open ended questions and allow you time to respond.

The session will generally last between 20 minutes to an hour. At its conclusion, the hypnotherapist will bring you slowly back to the present where you will be awakened.

It's been my experience that the hypnotherapist will give you the post-hypnotic suggestion so that you will awake fully refreshed. At that time, you will become fully conscious and feel like you just had a spa date. Take just a moment to absorb and understand your experience as you return to fully being present in the moment.

Even in the deepest moments of hypnotic relaxation, you will have full control of your body. If at any time you feel uncomfortable, you can wake yourself during the session. If you force yourself awake, it can be jarring experience but at any time you feel the need to return or want to be present, you can.

If you feel distressed at any time during your session, the hypnotherapist, who will be monitoring you; will remind you that you are an observer of any traumatic event, and instruct you to watch your past life as a spectator. In almost all instances, you will be able to watch the experience calmly. If you are unable to do this, the hypnotherapist will bring you back to the present or end the session.

If you feel uncomfortable or uneasy about the process, bring in a friend to monitor your session and record notes. They will be welcomed and told to sit quietly.

Dr Brian Weiss, has some wonderful meditation regressions CDs on past life recall. They include *Regression through the Mirrors of Time, Many Lives, Many Masters* and *Through Time into Healing.* I recommend Dr. Weiss's CDs, his classes, live presentations and his books. Dr. Weiss is truly amazing and his CDs give you a guided and a very gentle access to your past lives.

As stated, I recommend going to a licensed professional for a past life regression. Dr. Weiss's CDs and tapes will also work for you.

There can be much to learn and experience in a past life regression, but remember while entertaining and interesting, your primary goal is to live your current life fully; not get lost in a previous one.

Chapter 10
Cord Cutting Past Lives

On occasion, there seems as if something is holding you back from achieving your desires. It's not quite tangible, but you know it's there, blocking your good. We may not be cognizant of the cause, but we know we are experiencing the effect. Whatever it is, its holding you back.

Some will dismiss the uneasiness as Mercury in retrograde. Those who understand quantum physics want to define the cause and take corrective measures to steady their course.

That illusive something which is holding you back may be an Etherical Cord. An Etherical Cord binds us to a forgotten experience in our current life or even a past life.

Etheric cords connect us to people, places, animals, things and events. They ribbon their way through time to vows, pledges and promises we made in a past life.

I see etherical cords as thin, fine, shimmering, silvery, tubing that glitters and sparkles between ourselves and those we love. You may not be able to see these etherical cords but you can feel them. We have all felt the tug of an etherical cord when we sense a loved one is in danger. They pull at our heartstrings when something deep inside you urges you to call a friend or loved one.

These cords also bind us to experiences, places, and things.

Etheric cords can manifest in fears and unknown phobias such as a fear of falling, fire or open water. Soldiers who experience PTSD are thrown back into horrific moment of combat by the backfire of a car.

A past client of mine was tied to a horrible motorcycle accident he experienced as a teen. He was held to the incident by a strong etherical cord.

Etherical Cords can stretch to previous lifetimes where we made vows of poverty or chastity. We spoke our oaths with such deep sincerity, they are now showing up in our current life where they manifest as self-sabotaging behavior in our financials and relationships.

I made such a vow in the 12th century. Through a past life regression, I saw and experienced my life as a monk. I cut that binding cord and released my vow of poverty.

Unhealthy cords can manifest as feelings of depression, melancholy, obsessive thoughts and behaviors. We can experience these cords when they twist from their original intent into unhealthy eating or drinking patterns; perhaps a carryover from a time when we experienced starvation or famine.

I have seen some individuals who have an instant addiction and connection to drugs or alcohol. Their instant connection to substance abuse may not be from a physical weakness in this life but dates back to in time when they abused substances. If any of these words or experiences resonate within you, there may be a cord that needs to be cut.

The act of cutting a cord does not have to be a complicated ceremonial event, in fact, it can be a simple visualization and take only minutes.

There are many types of cord-cutting techniques on the internet. Find one that feels natural to you.

The following is a cord-cutting, I use and have found to be very effective.

In my practice, I work with Angels, so I call on Archangel Michael and Archangel Raphael. Archangel Michael appears as a warrior angel with a fiery sword. Archangel Raphael is the healer Angel and works with doctors, medical practitioners and healers. He is often seen with a beautiful emerald green light.

Remember the Angels are always ready to help you.

How to do a Past Life Cord Cutting through Visualization

1. Pick a time when you will not be disturbed.

2. Slowly close your eyes and visualize yourself in a safe place. This place is one of your choosing. You can choose a beach, waterfall, or any serene vista in   which you feel at peace.

3. Breathe in to the count of 8. Hold that breath to a count of 3 and then   release it slowly to the count of 8. This type of breathing is called yoga breaths.   As you breathe in, take in pure white light, hold the breath for 3 seconds and then slowly release it to the count of 8; releasing any worries, stress or any negative thoughts inside you. Do this until you feel "clean".

4. Invite Archangel Michael and Archangel Raphael

to be you. They will instantly appear and you feel protected and safe in their presence.

5. You are now ready to cut and release any etherical cords that bind you.

Say: *"I release all vows of poverty, celibacy or chastity that I may have made in a previous life that no longer serve me. I call on Archangel Michael to sever any cords   created in a past life that bind me to negative experiences or emotions. I release any fears, doubts, feelings of unworthiness, self-denial, self-punishment or any self-sabotaging behavior that was born from any past life trauma. I release any karmic debt that causes me pain or suffering. All effects of those vows and the karmic debt are healed. I no longer suffer the effects of any past choices which block me or keep me from my good. Going forward, I strengthen my cords of love to those who love me and whom I love. I awaken the ancient wisdom within me. I am now open to a beautiful new life filled with more love, more joy, more health, more abundance than I have ever known or experienced. And so, it is."*

6. Archangel Michael stands at the ready with his burning sword and in one sweeping movement severs the offending cord. You watch the cord dissolve into   wisps of nothingness.

7. With the cord cut, ask Archangel Raphael to salve the wound with his green healing light.

8. A soothing calm washes over you and your return to the present, feeling fully awake, fully rested and open to any gifts, knowledge or talents you have   awakened in this ceremony.

9. Close your visualization by saying, *"Thank you,*

Father-Mother-God, for the release of any etherical cords that no longer serve me".

Use these words or substitute your own words.

For some etherical cords, a single cord-cutting will suffice. Other cords may be stronger and will regrow. If that is the case, repeat the cord-cutting and create a positive affirmation to support your new way of thinking.

You will know your cord cutting is successful, when you no longer think about a person, place or thing. You may find your finances are improving or you are able to experience day to day life without any obsessive thoughts.

As I mentioned, I work with Angels and I also use crystals to aid me. Crystals are found in communication devices from computers, cell phones and satellites. Crystals can also help you connect with the Divine.

For a cord cutting, I like to recommend holding a crystal such as Black Tourmaline, Rose Quartz and Petrified Wood.

Black Tourmaline is good for grounding, calming the mind and body as well as releasing and repelling negative energy. Black Tourmaline will also assist in transforming any dense energy into a higher or lighter vibration.

Rose Quartz carries within its feelings of love and forgiveness. Many people also use Rose Quartz when working with the heart chakra. Rose Quartz promotes healing and feelings of peace. Its healing properties include filling you with kindness and compassion toward others and yourself.

Smoky Quartz is also member of the Quartz family

that supports grounding and helps to cleanse and detoxify your mind and body.

Petrified Wood is known for deep spiritual connections, helps you with grounding and stabilizes your energy.

You do not need to obtain all of the crystals mentioned but choose the ones that resonate with you.

If you are looking for a quality source of crystals, I highly recommend Debbie Hardy. She is a trusted source of high quality but very affordable crystals and offers a wide variety of crystals to choose. Debbie is an author, Certified Crystal Healer, Advanced Crystal Master and Reiki Master. You can contact Debbie through her website at www.hardycrystalblessing.com.

If you feel you need to contact a professional, there are wonderful psychics and lightworkers who can assist you in cord-cutting. Do a google search and of course, I recommend reading their reviews.

Keep the loving, beautiful cords that bind you to your loved ones but cut any cords that keep you from experiencing your good.

Chapter 11
The Akashic Records

The Akashic Records is the repository of our every thought, word, and deed, feeling, as well the energy behind our feelings and emotions. The Akashic Records are the central storehouse of all information for every individual who has ever lived upon the earth. Each of us has our own personal Akashic Record also known as the Book of Life.

The Akashic Records are also known as "The Book of Life" or "God's Book of Remembrance." References of the Akashic Records or the Book of Life are found in both the New and Old Testaments.

Psalm 56:8-9, in the Tanakh Bible, the passage reads "You keep count of my wanderings; into your record."

In the New Jerusalem Bible, it is written in, Psalm 139:16, "You had scrutinized my every action, all were recorded in your book, my days listed and determined, even before the first of them occurred."

Information and the study of The Akashic Records dates back to the Assyrians and Babylonians.

Buddhists refer to the Akashic Records as the Alaya Consciousness, which translates to the storehouse of limitless consciousness.

At the turn of the 19th century, Helena Blavatsky, one of the founders of the Theosophical Movement, shared she first learned of the Akashic Records from Tibetan

Monks.

Edgar Cayce, the most documented psychic of all time, helped thousands of people through his remarkable ability to access a patient's Akashic Records. From the patient's history and recorded health records, Cayce successfully diagnosed and recommend treatment.

To provide you a modern-day analogy of the Akashic Records, I ask you to envision a massive multiplex movie complex where all the shows are about you and are accessible at all times. The first theater could be is a film of your toddler years, in the next a movie you could find a showing of your preteen years followed by screening of your life's story to the present. Other viewings depict future lives. All time is now. All movies are running concurrently. You choose what you want to view or experience.

Another example of how the Akashic Records can be found in the scroll bar on a YouTube video or a Netflix film. On the screen you will find a scrubber, scrub bar or sometimes referred to as seek bar at the bottom of a screen. You click on the play icon to view the video. When you hit the pause, the video will stop. To reengage, you click resume, and your video will move forward. If you want to fast forward, you simply drag the scroll to the end of the scrub bar.

The ball on the scrubber indicates where you are at the present moment. You control the icon to move forward in the video or move back.

This is the same when you access the Akashic Records. You can view your past, or see your future life to understand the consequences of your actions. Remember you have the ability to change your future by decisions you make each day.

Imagine a film crew following you every day, recording your every thought and the energy behind each emotion and action. As incredible as this sounds, this description gives you a very accurate representation of the Akashic Records.

Metaphysicians, as well as Mom and Dad, tell you to pay attention to your words and your thoughts. Every moment of your life builds onto the next moment and fashions your outcomes. You are the creator of your life.

At one time, the Akashic Records were believed to be accessible only to a few spiritual clerics known as the Akashic Record Keepers. Most of us today refer to ourselves as Akashic Record Readers.

The Akashic Records store not only our individual records but they keep a record of world history.

Through the Akashic Records we have access to our past lives, our current life as well as the future. The future is not carved in stone, for by changing our thoughts we can course correct and create a different outcome.

The Akashic Records can help you in solving and resolving relationship issues and financial patterns. We can change the past in the Akashic Records and thereby altering the future.

I was able to rewrite my own past through the Akashic Records. I accomplished this by accessing my records. Through visualization, I went back to a time in my life when I was being mistreated, stepped into the records as my adult self, protected the child I once was. I told my parents to never hurt me again. I told my younger self that she was treasured and valued by a loving God.

Through my visualizations, I removed the energic patterns of the physical and mental abuse from my past. Today, I no longer recall these events or have any emotional attachment to them. I was able to fully forgive my parents and continue to treat myself with love and respect.

By identifying these memories, I eliminated them from my current life. With these karmic energies resolved. With the lessons, I do not have to repeat them in the future.

Through the Akashic Records you can find healing in your current life with relationships as well as alter, remove and release behaviors to include fears, blocks and phobias.

Through the Akashic Records you can gain insight on former talents from a past life or be open to new interests or passions.

To learn more about the Akashic Records or to become an Akashic Record Reader, I highly recommend my teacher, Sandra Anne Taylor. She offers classes through Hay House offers some of the most wonderful books on *The Akashic Records,* and other books on quantum physics. I also highly recommend her Oracle and Tarot Cards decks.

If you would like to work with an Akashic Record reader, you can easily find a certified reader though an internet search. Right now, I am working on my books, but I may reopen my practice on the Akashic Records. I am also a certified Crystal, Angel Card Reader and Angelic Life Coach. Before you register with any psychic, medium or Akashic Record Reader, read their reviews.

The following is a how-to exercise to help you access your Akashic Records through visualization.

I will leave you with an outline of the techniques at the end of this chapter but first I want to share some tips to help you on your journey.

Though I have shared a disclaimer at the beginning of this book. I am going to repeat it here per legal requirements. This book is an overview of past lives and exploration into the world of reincarnation. All visualizations offered and meditations shared with you are for education and entertainment. The visualizations and meditations are not be taken as medical advice. If you need to see a doctor, or medical professional do so.

Accessing Your Akashic Records thru Visualization

Before you begin to access your Akashic Records, I have a couple of dos and don'ts. These are suggestions to help enhance your experience.

It's not mandatory but I believe it helps you set the stage by lighting a candle or using a salt lamp. I like the peace and calming effect of either.

Crystals are optional. I work with crystals and I find them helpful when I meditate or do a visualization.

I'd like to suggest you hold one or two Black Tourmaline for grounding, calming the mind and body as well as releasing and repelling negative energy. Black Tourmaline will also assist in transforming any dense energy into a higher or lighter vibration.

Rose Quartz brings with it, feelings of love and forgiveness. Its healing properties include kindness and compassion and will help you forgive yourself and others.

Smoky Quartz is a member of the Quartz family that supports grounding and helps to cleanse and detoxify both mind and body.

Petrified Wood also helps in grounding as well as it has a stabilizing effect on your energy.

I use Tangerine Orange Crystals to help me with the Akashic Records and accessing past lives. Tangerine Orange Crystal also helps in releasing feelings of guilt and regret. They are a powerhouse when accessing past lives.

As mentioned previously, I recommend Debbie Hardy as a reliable source for crystals. Her crystals are of very good quality and she is extremely knowledgeable.

Setting the stage also includes selecting a quiet time. This is a visualization, so you will not be in a deep meditative or hypnotic state. I do recommend you set aside a block of time when you will not be disturbed.

As you prepare to go into your meditative state, write down your intention. You can place your intention before you or under a crystal. Writing out your intention is like having a bus ticket to an exact destination. Without an intention or goal, your Akashic Record guide will assist you in access the information that would be most beneficial for this journey into time.

Write your intention. You question in this session can be question such as what is the source of my money issues or is there anything I need to learn about my relationship with i.e., Mathew.

In the meditative state, an Akashic Record Guide will appear to you as you enter the Great Hall of Records. Your guide can be an Angel, or Divine Guardian. Whoever comes forward will serve as you in accessing your Akashic Records.

Next get comfortable. Close your eyes and visualize a safe peaceful place. Do some deep yoga breaths. The purpose of this is to clear out and release any negative energy or anxiety you might be feeling. Your special safe place could be a beach, by a waterfall, in a serene valley or a wooded glen. It's your safe place.

Do yoga breathes. Breathe in to the count of 8. Hold the breath for a count of 3 and then release it to the count of 8. You should feel your tummy rise and fall as you take in and release these in deep breaths.

As you breathe in take in beautiful pure white light, hold it, see the divine light, swirling within you, collecting any negative emotions. When you are ready, breath out allowing these emotions to dissipate into whiffs of dark smoke before they dissolve into the nothingness they are.

Let go of worries of what to feed the family for dinner or the lives of TV reality. This is about you. Clear and quiet your mind. Release any thoughts other than the love and peace you feel in you, around you, above you and below you. Do this for several minutes.

As you enter the meditative state, ground myself with crystals in each palm. Feel roots travel from your feet deep into the earth until you feel very safe and fully anchored.

Open yourself to receive the Divine White Light

of the Universe and call out to Archangel Michael to assist you. Michael is a powerful Archangel, who makes appearances in the Bible, the Torah and the Quran. He is usually pictured with his flaming sword. Michael is our great protector as well as the patron saint of law enforcement and the military. Michael is always ready to assist all who call upon him.

You don't need a formal prayer or invocation to bring Michael to you, simply say, *"Archangel Michael, I ask that you protect me as I enter the great hall of the Akashic Records. I ask you to watch over me in this journey."*

The Akashic Records is a library of vibrational energy. I give it form as it aids me in my visualization. In my mind's eye, I see a massive Greek-Roman style structure that houses within it more books than I can count.

As you enter the great hall, a Guide will warmly greet you. Your guide may be an angel, a personal guardian, Jesus or an ancient philosopher. You don't need to conjure up who, the Guide best suited for you and your purposes will appear.

Your Guide will take you to a section that, is devoted to you. Together you will open a scroll or volume in which you will find the answer or insight you seek.

You can view your records though various mediums such as an ancient scroll, a book or a holographic movie screen. I see my records in a book form and once the book is opened, my records are projected into a holographic image of light and emotion.

Allow the imagery to appear before you. As this record of your past life unfolds, observe and learn. If you see something is disturbing or frightens you, leave or ask your guide to show you another account.

My visits to the Akashic Records are, for the most part relatively short, you can come back and visit any time. Note as the days pass, you will intuitively acquire more memories of that life to include a greater understanding of your issue and more patience and compassion from this revelation.

When you feel you are complete with your viewing, thank your Guide. Take any information or recommendations your Guide shares with you.

Slowly return to your present and say thank you to God, the Universe. Allow a warm feeling of gratitude to wash over your body.

I'd like to suggest your write down your experience to include any insights you may have gain.

Create an affirmation for yourself such as, "*I forgive myself and that person or experience for the pain or hurt I endured. I am no longer bound by any past mistakes, toxic patterns or experiences from past lives. I create a beautiful new experience by honoring myself every day. And so, It Is!*"

As I close this chapter, I want to direct you to Sandra Anne Taylor, most notably her book *The Akashic Records* for more in-depth information and knowledge.

My goal in this book is to give you an overview of reincarnation, The Akashic Records and to instill in you a desire to learn more.

The following is a summary of what I have shared to make it make it easier for you to follow the instructions I have laid out in this chapter.

Visualization Summary

1. Set the Stage. Select a quiet time. Use Crystals and Candles as you prefer.
2. Write out your intention.
3. Still your mind. Do yoga breaths to release negative energy or busy thoughts.
4. Call on Archangel Michael to help and protect you.
5. Ground yourself.
6. Go to a meditative state of total relaxation.
7. Go into the Great Hall where you will be greeted by your Guide.
8. With your Guide, go to your Akashic Records.
9. Be open to witnessing what you are shown with understanding and clarity
10. When you are complete, thank your Guide
11. Slowly return to your place and your body. You are refreshed
12. Record your journey and what information you gained.
13. If needed, write an affirmation to use with this new insight
14. In the days that follow, be open to receiving greater insights.

If you are interested in past lives only, I refer you to the chapter on past lives.

The Akashic Records may give you more information that you want to learn.

Chapter 12
Frequently Asked Questions on Reincarnation

The following are frequently asked questions about Reincarnation. The answers are my own based on my research, and study as well as my own past life experiences.

I hope my insights light your way to a deeper understanding of Reincarnation.

The following are questions I have answered over the years. If you have questions, please feel free to contact me at LinnRandom@thebusinessisde.blog.

How many years pass between incarnations?

Some souls, especially if their death was sudden or their lives cut short, will reincarnate immediately.

Most people have come to a more common consensus that there are at least 20 years between lives. Hindus believe the life cycle is about 49 days.

Your chose when you want to reincarnate.

My previous life before my current incarnation was over 100 years ago. Some choose to incarnate at 500-year intervals or even longer.

A soul can incarnate in their group, skip a generation or two or incarnate with an entirely new group.

There is much to do and explore on the other side.

The choice is always yours.

Do all souls reincarnate?

No. Some souls choose to remain in the spirit realm to learn and explore other worlds or support and assist those on an earthly path.

Why do we reincarnate?

We choose to reincarnate to learn lessons of love, compassion, and forgiveness. We choose to incarnate to balance our karma and support other souls on their life journeys.

We choose to incarnate to become closer to God, the Universe.

Why don't people remember past lives?

While past life recall, especially your own, is fun and interesting, most people do not remember past lives because we are not meant to remember them.

Past lives give us insight into our current lives, but again, we are not meant to remember past lives.

We are meant to focus on this life and the lessons we have come here to learn and balance our karmic energy.

Is Reincarnation an unavoidable process?

It's up to you. From a human perspective, you might be inclined to respond, I'm not doing this again. You will have an entirely different perspective in the spirit realm. It's going to be up to you as to whether you reincarnate.

I only recall just short moments of previous lives.

That's okay. It's not necessary to recall a past life in its entirety. Even small glimpses can be sufficient to answer your questions or gain insight into experiences.

I have found that once the door is opened to a past life, other memories will come in the days and weeks following a past life regression.

Will I reincarnate as an animal?

In my opinion and the opinion of many others, we do not believe we reincarnate to animals. Humans have a higher intelligence and again it is my opinion, we would not reincarnate into life with less intellect.

Some believers feel we can incarnate into an animal species but there are no past life regressions that support this that I am aware of.

Do animals have souls?

Yes, animals have beautiful souls. Animals have amazing insight, compassion and have learned to love unconditionally. They have exquisite souls.

Will my pet return to me?

There are many stories about a new puppy or kitten displaying the same characteristics or personalities similar to former pets. Some pets even have similar markings. Sadly, not all pets return to former owners.

It has not happened to me but I hope your beloved companions finds their way back to you.

Is there a purpose an innocent man spending their life in jail?

If a prisoner is wrongly convicted of a crime, finds himself or herself in jail, from a perspective of the oversoul, there may be a life lesson to learn.

We can speculate that a person may have sent an innocent to jail or took another's life without being held liable in that lifetime. Karma will be balanced.

The objective of such a lesson would be to forgive all, release any anger or injustice associated with the incarceration and find peace.

An alternative mission might be for the wrongly convicted person to fight for justice.

Either way, there is a life lesson in this experience and karma will be balanced.

Can I change genders?

Yes. You can change genders as you may want to

experience life through the prism of male and or female viewpoints. For example, you may want to explore parental roles as a Mother in one life; you have the choice to return into another life as a father.

You choose your gender based on your soul's highest growth and experiences through different perspectives.

Is homosexuality a choice?

Yes, like gender homosexuality is a choice. Your choice of sexual preference depends on what you wish to experience.

It is your responsibility and obligation to love everyone unconditionally.

What about the transgender person who comes to earth as male then changes their sex to female?

Modern medicine allows humans the opportunity to change their genders midlife. This provides a totally unique experience to the individual soul.

The lesson may be to experience life as both male and female. The lesson may be for those around them to accept their loved one's choices by offering them unconditional love.

How do we recognize our soulmates, friends, family and others?

We intuitively connect to our friends, soulmates and even coworkers but at the soul level through vibrational energy. It's not the physical appearance we recognize, it's the vibration and energic patterns.

We have all seen dogs who are immediately wary of one person and then happily greet another. A dog picks on the energy of strangers and people around them.

We also intuitively recognize the energy in others. After a bad relationship, we can look back and say with 20/20 hindsight, I knew in my gut there was something wrong with that person. Why didn't I listen to myself? Why indeed?

In the spirit realm, NDEs share they recognize their 80-year-old grandmother as the woman they knew in their lives or are able to recognize her as 35-year-old woman she wishes to project.

NDEs have also shared that they meet friends or family who may have been missing a limb in their past life are fully restored in the spirit realm. Those who needed a wheelchair in this life are now standing.

Children and toddlers who passed are waiting to greet them as adults.

Why do some souls choose to reincarnate to be evil?

Some souls volunteer incarnates to do evil. These people can be part of our soul's experience and part of our soul's growth.

What about Hitler?

It's challenging to view Hitler without judgement as he was responsible for the death and torture of over 8 million Jews and others, he deemed unsuitable for life.

Karma will always be balanced. In the case of Hitler, karma may be balanced by experiencing millions of individual tortuous deaths. Add to that total, how the death of each lost soul was experienced by a loved one. Now calculate into this karmic debt, the sufferings left by soldiers in their wake as well as all who experienced famine, rape or hardships because of his ambitions. Suffice to say, the debt is immeasurable and staggering.

Do no evil. Karma will be balanced.

Where do new souls come from?

There are two decidedly different schools of thought on this subject.

The first group believes all souls were created at one time which folds into a big bang theory. The second line of thought is that the Universe is ever expanding in whereby new souls are being created.

You can choose your own answer, for me, it's simply a question I will ask on the other side.

Do we dream of past lives?

I believe that past lives can be experienced or lived concurrently through dreams.

Dreams that are exceptionally vivid and rich in color with historic context may very well be memories of a past life.

Recurring dreams such as falling, being chased can

be manifestations of past life experiences.

If you are experiencing repeated nightmares, I would recommend they be addressed, healed or purged from your mind. This is especially true if the dream interferes with your waking life.

I suggest you identify the source cause by either working with a licensed therapist or do a past life regression with a certified professional. Either way, uncover the cause and release.

Dreams are also a way of exploring other worlds or work through current life problems.

If you are curious about your dreams, record them and look for patterns or messages from your subconscious mind.

When do I enter my mother's body?

You enter your mother's body at the time you choose.

Some souls incarnate and experience the entire gestation. Others choose to enter the child's body at birth. Some souls may wait and enter the physical body a few days after the birth.

It will depend on the soul's desires and agenda. Souls will choose the optimum time for the soul's greatest good.

What about Suicide?

There is no burning hell waiting for a person who commits suicide.

However, as you understand the laws of Karma, what does await is repeating the entire life sequence over in a future life. The next experience could be more painful. Not only will the soul go through their own personal pain again but will experience the pain and anguish of those they left behind.

Its far better to rise above the circumstances than repeat the life experience again.

Suicide is a permanent solution to a temporary problem.

If you or you know of someone who is contemplating suicide call the National Suicide Prevention Lifeline at 800-273-8255.

Do you believe in heaven?

Yes, but allow me to clarify. For me, this heavenly realm is not filled with streets of gold or endless mansions.

My vision of this spirit world is filled with exceptional art, magnificent landscapes with colors our human minds cannot yet perceive. In my view heaven is filled with all sorts of opportunities to learn. In this world, we can visit other planets or become guides or guardian angels to help others.

Do you believe in hell?

No. As mentioned earlier in this book, the early Christian Church believed in reincarnation. They did not believe in hell. At the Council of Nicaea, the church leaders changed the original texts to better suit their narrative.

When Jesus spoke of hell, he was speaking of hell torment of the mind, not a burning hell to be suffered after a single lifetime on earth.

For more information on this, I urge you to study the Aramaic Bible, which was the language of Jesus. The Aramaic Bible is a book of love and a loving God, not a book of judgement and condemnation.

There have been thousands of NDEs accounts, not one has reported or saw evidence of a burning hell.

NDE accounts all state of being greeted by a loving and compassionate being. This same scenario is also reported by atheists who go through a near death experience.

When I encounter someone who believes in hell, I offer no judgements or try to dissuade them overwise. I say, "if you want to believe in hell, you can. I chose not to."

What do you think about parallel lives?

A Parallel life is a theory that two people live different lives at the same time.

This idea may sound like something straight out of a sci-fi novel but some people believe it to be true.

I have no experience in this subject nor do I know

any others who do.

However, I will point out as atoms can be split; fertile eggs can be divided so perhaps our energy can split to maximize our experience here on earth.

I am not aware of any parallel lives and have no knowledge of this subject. One could speculate such a theory is possible.

What if my soul mate is no longer in my life?

If your soul mate or life partner is no longer with you on the earth plane, it maybe they have chosen different lessons to experience. Perhaps part of your lesson is to go on with your life, understanding the loss and loneliness that comes after of losing a loved one.

If your soulmate has transitioned to the spirit realm, it may be your partners has moved on and so should you. There are many experiences ahead of everyone as well as new loving relationships explore. Be assured you are still connected with them and they will be waiting for you on the other side.

In the meantime, I can assure you, it is their wish and desire that you go on with your life and experience all good things. Your partner in this life would certainly want you to experience love and companionship again.

Love is forever.

Why do infants and children die?

This is the hardest of questions to answer and the one that began my journey into reincarnation.

To shed light on this hard subject, our examination and understanding should begin through the perspective of the oversoul. Death is not real. We do not die. The child does not die. The child lives, we live and we will be joined with our beloved child again.

Looking through this experience through the prism of reincarnation, both the soul of the child and the parents agreed to undergo this life experience. Our understanding is limited as to why the soul of a child choose to have a short life or why the parents choose to suffer such unspeakable pain. I can only speculate it may have been important for their souls to understand grief, heartache and rise above such enormous grief.

For me, my child loss came with the lesson that life is to be valued. In my own journey, I had not cherished life in other lifetimes and have a painful memory of the lives I took. As I came to understand this, my lesson was learned and my karmic debt absolved. Through the Law of Grace, I am grateful to share, I had the son I so desperately wanted.

For the child, the infant or toddler their life lesson was to be part of this experience and to embrace parental love for a short period of time.

Full clarity will come in the spirit realm as will the knowingness that you will one day hold your child again.

Why do some people believe they were Anne Boleyn or Marilyn Monroe?

Anne Boleyn was the second Queen of Henry VIII of England. There are many people who have experienced similar tragic love stories and emotionally link with their lives to hers.

I suspect some who claim they are the reincarnation of Queen Anne Boleyn, without a past life regression, may have actually lived during her lifetime. Her story was so prominent at the time, they embrace her life as their own.

At the moment, I am aware of four women now who believe they are the reincarnation of Marilyn Monroe. Is it possible that one of them is Ms. Monroe? I don't know nor do I even want to speculate. Again, there are many women and perhaps men who relate to her story.

If you believe you are the reincarnation of Napoleon or another famous or infamous personage of history, I'm perfectly okay with that.

For me and the rest of us, we have lived ordinary lives across time, loving, learning lessons for our souls highest good.

Can everyone be hypnotized?

Not everyone can be hypnotized. Studies indicate that 10% of us are naturally resistant to a hypnosis. Research states that another 10% of us who are highly susceptible and leaving approximately 80% of people who are moderately inclined.

If you feel like you want to explore a past life regression or hypnosis, I recommend go to a psychiatrist or licensed hypnotherapist.

If you just want to explore or get some basic information, a CD, video or self-hypnosis techniques will generally get you into a nice relaxed meditative state where you can obtain general answers and information you seek.

Can I experience a past life regression using a CD?

Yes, Dr. Brian Weiss has several CDs that will walk you through the process of a past life regression. Dick Sutphen also has CDs available.

There are others in the market, I am most familiar with Dr. Weiss and Dick Sutphin's and have success with both. Many others are available to you.

I've seen people come who cluck like a chicken. Can my hypnotherapist make me do that?

If you are open to the suggestion, there is a possibility but for the most part those who give such a ridiculous suggestion are stage hypnotists. I would never agree to be part of a stage performance, nor would I ever suggest you be part of such exportation.

For this type of suggestions to work your mind must be willing to accept this type of suggestion. Your mind will reject anything you deem as foolish or dangerous.

You can awaken yourself from any hypnotherapy session at any time if you wish. In a hypnotherapy session you are relaxed and fully aware of what your hypnotherapist is saying.

If you are still concerned, take a friend with you to

any hypnotherapy session.

Is it possible to go into future lives?

Yes. You can gain information about your future through the Akashic Records.

A psychic or an oracle card or Akashic Record reader can provide you with information about the future.

Keep in mind, the Psychic or Tarot or Oracle Card Reader, are offering information based on your current energy. If you think different thoughts, change patterns or your interactions with another you also shift the future.

Your future is determined by decisions you make each day.

.

Tell me about your other books in this series?

Manifestation through Affirmations and Visualization explains how to use the Law of Attraction to bring your desires and wishes to the manifest plane. I also go in-depth as to why affirmations or prayers don't work as well as how to combine energy with visualization to manifest your goals and desires.

My book, *Etherical Cords and Cord Cutting* goes into greater depth on Etherical cords. In this book, I will explain how to recognize them and understand their effect in your life. *Etherical Cords and Cord Cutting* will describe how to cut these cords and free yourself from limiting beliefs, promises and vows you may have made in past lives as well as obsessive ties you have to people or events that keep you from experiencing your best life.

Both of these books will be available early summer of 2021.

If you are in a new age business, I'd like to introduce you to my book *The Business Side of a Spiritual Practice*. This book is a how to market and promote your spiritual business online and in the real work from event marketing to how to write a business plan and promotional calendar to keep you in the buzz year-round. This book is available on Amazon.com and can also be found at Balboa Press, a division of Hay House.

You can find more information about my romance's novels, romantic suspense novels, comedies and paranormal novels on my website www.Linn Random.com.

Chapter 13
In Conclusion

It is not necessary to understand past lives, any more than it is to understand what you did on a particular day in 1967.

This book is intended as an introduction to the concepts of reincarnation and perhaps answer a few questions.

If you would like to understand more, and I hope you do, I'd like to recommend the following books, chapters, crystals, classes and CDs.

Recommended Reading

In addition to the books listed below, I recommend any and all books by Dr. Raymond Moody, Brian Weiss, and James Van Praagh.

I encourage you to continue your study and interest in past lives to understand there is no death, only life, after life, after life.

To understand karma and the need to rise above it through forgiveness and love and release.

Hypnotherapy is not for cocktail parties or play-dates with friends. If you decided to do experience a past life regression, do so with a licensed hypnotherapist or a certified Akashic Record Reader.

To explore topics of interest, I recommend the following books.

The Search for Bridey Murphy by Morey Bernstein

Reincarnation and Karma by Edgar Cayce

Embraced by the Light by Betty J. Eadie

Life After Life by Dr. Raymond Moody

Adventures of the Soul by James van Praagh

Signs from Pets In The Afterlife by Lyn Ragan

You Were Born Again to Be Together by Dick Sutphen

The Akashic Records by Sandra Anne Taylor

Return to Life: Extraordinary Cases of children Who Remember Past Lives by, Dr. Jim Tucker

Many Lives, Many Masters by Brian Weiss

Crystals Recommendation

There are wonderful crystals available through many sources, I recommend crystals by Debbie Hardy for quality and affordable crystals.

www.hardycrystalblessing.com

About The Author

Linn Random is a Reincarnationist with over 40 years' experience in past life recall.

Linn also runs her own spiritual practice, Sacred Angel Therapy. She is a certified Angelic Life Coach, Fairy-ologist, and is an Akashic Record Reader, Certified Angelic Life Coach, Oracle Card Reader, and is Certified Crystal Healing.

Linn Random is a marketing and communications specialist with a comprehensive background in domestic and international marketing.

Her experience includes all aspects of Public Relations campaign and strategy, including Copy Writing, Event Planning, Media Kits and Public Relations.

When she first retired, she was the National Director of an International Marketing firm, and in the mid-1990s, she was Executive Vice-President of a major Internet Company and became involved in all aspects of marketing and promotion on the world wide web.

You are invited to view Linn Randoms' online class on *Reincarnation a Journey of the Soul* at Udemy.com.

Romantic Suspense Novels

Linn Random has loved romantic suspense since she watched Snow White run from the woodcutter's ax into the arms of a handsome Prince.

Her Romance Novels offer readers spine-tingling suspense, action-packed excitement, and characters that sparkle with intensity and emotion. Reviews state over and over that her novels are fresh, with multilayered plots.

Linn Random has been a frequent guest speaker at groups such as Sisters in Crime, numerous chapters of the Romance Writers of America, the Florida Writers Association, the Mystery Writers of America's Sleuthfest, and has taught online classes.

Linn lives in Central Florida with her husband and two dogs, Wally, and Bae.

For more information about Linn, visit

www.LinnRandom.com

Printed in Great Britain
by Amazon